This
Whitaker Playhouse
Book Belongs to:

In Him was life; and the life was the light of men.

John 1:4

Scripture quotations marked (KJVER) are taken from the *King James Easy Read Bible*, KJVER®, © 2001, 2007, 2010, 2015 by Whitaker House. Used by permission. All rights reserved.

The Story of the Good Samaritan
www.philsmouse.com
ISBN: 978-1-64123-612-6
© 2021 by Phil A. Smouse

Whitaker House
1030 Hunt Valley Circle
New Kensington, PA 15068
www.whitakerhouse.com

1 2 3 4 5 6 7 8 9 10 11 LU 28 27 26 25 24 23 22 21

THE STORY OF THE GOOD SAMARITAN

if you love the wonderful, rollicking rhythm and rhyme of the classic picture books you read as a child and want to bring that same sense of joy to your children, you're in the right place.

Learning, understanding, and living God's Word is a journey that lasts a lifetime. And that journey starts by reading God's Word. Every tiny heart on the face of this earth is trying to find its way home to Jesus. And God's eternal promise to our precious little lambs is that they will find Him—when we take the time to show them how and where to look.

Jesus wants us to be His—one hundred percent. And the most important thing is not what we say or do, or even who we reach. The most important thing is the relationship we cultivate with Him.

That deep spiritual connection isn't only for adults. The truths you share with your children from God's Word will stay with them for the rest of their lives. This delightful, child-friendly Bible story is a perfect way to introduce those precious little ones to the joy of a heart filled with Jesus and the knowledge of God's Word.

Phil A. Smouse

You shall love your neighbor as yourself.
Matthew 22:39

"A walk," I thought. "Now, that sounds nice—

like paradise to be precise.
To Jericho. Yes, that will be
the thing to do today for me!"

But, oh my word, I never knew.
I never even had a clue
my jog-for-joy would turn into
a rendezvous with *you-know-who!*

You don't know who? Oh, sure you do.
I'll bet your Grandma knows him, too!

I strolled along. I sniffed the breeze.
Aaah, chamomile and peonies!
Yes, columbine and hollyhocks—
sweet lavender and creeping phlox.

Oh bliss! Oh joy! Oh, hybrid teas,
all borne upon the balmy breeze,
with honeysuckle—strawberries—
magnolia trees and. . .

stinky cheese?

STINKY CHEESE!? Say what?   Oh please!
Oh yes—the cheese that makes you *sneeze*.
Le-pew! Le-yuk! Le-hack! Le-wheeze!
Le-dirty, denim dungarees!

"Oh dear!" thought me. "What could it be?"
And then I spun around to see. . .

Two big, old, hairy, mean and scary
guys who any momentary
planned to take my happy day
and turn it 'round the other way!

They shook me up. They knocked me down.
They hauled me halfway back to town.
They snitched my clothes and snatched my cash.
They pulled and twisted my mustache.

Oh, Grandma told me not to go
down on the road to Jericho!

I tried to move, but nothing budged.
I'd been completely chocolate-fudged.
I needed help, to say the least.

That's when I saw the temple priest!

"Oh, icky poo. Now what is THAT
untidy mess?" the high-priest spat.

"That's really gross. How impolite,
to lay there right where I just might
be forced to look at such a sight.
Oh great, there goes my appetite."

And then with that, he took his feet,
and crossed them right across the street.

You're right. I should have been upset.
But listen, it's not over yet. . .

I heard the sound of soulful singing.
Psalms and hymns and tambo ringing.
Harps and zithers. Bells and whistles.
Holy rock and rolled epistles!

Man, I love that gospel sound!
That sound's the best dressed sound around.
And this guy, *he* could play it right.
THIS guy was really out of sight.

I guess he didn't see me there.
That must be why he didn't care
to stop and say, "How do you do?"
I would have stopped. Well, wouldn't *you?*

Of course you would. Of course you should.
Of course I fully understood,
that if you could you surely would,
but that won't do ME any good!

Who's *THAT*, you say? Who's *who?* Who's where?
OH NO! NOT THAT GUY OVER THERE!

When THAT guy gets a hold of me,
I'll be as boo-booed as can be!
I tell you, there has NEVER been
a truly good Samaritan.

Oh yes, I know. I'm so ashamed!
I never, *ever* should have blamed
that precious, tender, gentle man—
that godly, good Samaritan.

He patched up all my lumps and thumps.
He *bandaged* all my boo-boo bumps.
He rode me back on into town,
then picked me up and set me down—

yes, set me down without a sound
right in the best hotel around!

This cannot be! Not HIM— not ME.
This man's as puzzling as can be.

But he was warm, and true, and real.
He told me Jesus Christ could *heal*
my busted, broken, banged up heart. . .

I have loved you with an everlasting love.

Jeremiah 31:3

There's still more fun from Whitaker Playhouse.

Whitaker Playhouse

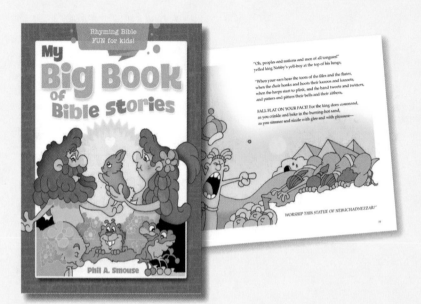

My Big Book of Bible Stories
978-1-64123-548-8

From award-winning author and illustrator Phil A. Smouse, *My Big Book of Bible Stories* features seventeen favorite Bible stories told in hilarious rhymes, with bright, full-color illustrations. These clever retellings of key Scriptures from the Old and New Testaments include the stories of creation, Adam and Eve, Jonah, the Good Samaritan, Jesus and Nicodemus, Peter, and more. Parents will enjoy reading *My Big Book of Bible Stories* to their preschool children, while young readers will delight in the whimsical story-telling and artwork.

My Big Book of Bible People, Places, and Things
978-1-64123-549-5

This brand-new Bible dictionary for kids features 750 entries with witty, age-appropriate text and colorful illustrations from award-winning author and illustrator Phil A. Smouse. *My Big Book of Bible People, Places, and Things* explains important terms in simple ways that young readers can easily grasp, while the full-color illustrations enhance your child's learning. With such entries as "Alleluia," "Book of Life," "Mary and Martha," and "Walking on Water," this book provides an important head start to scriptural literacy.

Bible ABCs   978-1-64123-428-3

Bible Activities   978-1-64123-430-6

Noah's Animals   978-1-64123-429-0

Bible 123s   978-1-64123-427-6

Away in a Manger   978-1-64123-527-3

Merry Christmas   978-1-64123-528-0

Wipe-Clean Activity Books

The *Inspired to Learn* series from Whitaker Playhouse is a perfect way for parents to share God's love with children while also introducing early learning concepts in a fun, interactive way.

These durable, wipe-clean books will provide hours of entertainment as children learn counting, the alphabet, color and shape recognition, drawing, spotting differences, and more. Parents will delight in their little one's progress as they enjoy the creative exercises.

WRITE TO PhiL A. SMOUSE

Once upon a time, Phil A. Smouse wanted to be a scientist.

But scientists don't get wonderful letters and pictures from friends like you. So Phil decided to draw and color instead! He and his wife live in sunny Lancaster, Pennsylvania. They have two married children, a granddaughter, and a goofy dog they love with all their heart.

Phil loves to tell kids like you all about Jesus. He would love to hear from you today! So get out your markers and crayons and send a letter or a picture to:

Phil A. Smouse
Whitaker House
1030 Hunt Valley Circle
New Kensington, PA 15068

Or visit his website at www.philsmouse.com
and send him an e-mail at: phil@philsmouse.com